JUN 2012

D1504978

Gilpin County Public Library

BIG GAME HUNTING

JUDY MONROE PETERSON

rosen publishing's
**rosen
central**

New York

Dave, you have inspired so many people, including me.

Published in 2011 by The Rosen Publishing Group, Inc.
29 East 21st Street, New York, NY 10010

Copyright © 2011 by The Rosen Publishing Group, Inc.

First Edition

All rights reserved. No part of this book may be reproduced in any form without permission in writing from the publisher, except by a reviewer.

Library of Congress Cataloging-in-Publication Data

Peterson, Judy Monroe.
Big game hunting / Judy Monroe Peterson. — 1st ed.
    p. cm. — (Hunting: pursuing wild game!)
Includes bibliographical references and index.
ISBN 978-1-4488-1240-0 (library binding) —
ISBN 978-1-4488-2270-6 (pbk.) —
ISBN 978-1-4488-2281-2 (6-pack)
1. Big game hunting—Juvenile literature. I. Title.
SK35.5.P48 2011
799.2'6—dc22

2010006859

Manufactured in Malaysia

CPSIA Compliance Information: Batch #W11YA: For further information, contact Rosen Publishing, New York, New York, at 1-800-237-9932.

On the cover: White-tailed deer can commonly be found in the eastern part of the United States.

CONTENTS

People all over the United States and Canada hunt large, wild animals called big game. They enjoy the challenge and excitement of matching wits with animals that are smart, fast, and well adapted to their environment. Most big game animals live in or near forests and lakes. Examples of big game animals are white-tailed deer, moose, elk, bear, and wild boar. Another type of deer, the mule deer, lives in mountains, foothills, prairies, and low brush lands. Some of the big game animals live only in specific regions of North America. Big game hunters feel a sense of pride and accomplishment after a successful hunt, plus they harvest delicious meat as food.

Hunting is an excellent way to explore nature, see different wildlife, and spend time outdoors. Hunters enjoy the physical and mental activity. They report a sense of well-being after spending time in the quiet of the woods—even when returning home without harvesting an animal. Big game hunting can be good exercise. Hunters typically walk miles over rugged land to get to and find an animal's habitat. If successful, they carry or drag the large, heavy animal back to their cabin, campsite, or vehicle.

People hunt big game animals for food to eat. The meat is lean, nutritious, and tasty. Most big game meat

Besides the time to enjoy natural scenery, the hunting of big game provides tasty meals and fun memories. Hunters often make lifelong friendships with their hunting partners.

is locally harvested, which saves natural resources. Other people use the hides, furs, bones, or horns of the animals to make useful items, such as clothing, shoes, boots, and belts. Jewelry, handbags, and other accessories are also made from these animals.

Often, groups of family members or friends hunt big game together year after year in the same area. They enjoy the companionship and the chance to bond with one another. In many families, hunting skills are passed through the generations. Still other people hunt for sport, or fun and recreation. They may preserve and display their animals.

Licensed hunters are important in the management and conservation of wildlife and natural habitats. They contribute to balancing wildlife populations. Big game hunters do not wipe out an entire population, and it is illegal to hunt animals that are endangered. Instead, people who hunt support laws to protect wildlife from extinction. They buy hunting licenses and pay special taxes on hunting equipment. This money helps pay for enforcement of hunting laws, wildlife management, and conservation programs. Most states do not have other ways to raise money for conservation. Many hunters donate their time to help with wildlife management projects, such as developing food and shelter habitats.

Wildlife is a publicly owned resource. Federal and state laws control hunting. The goal of these laws is to keep an expanded population of a certain animal from ruining a natural environment by overgrazing. The states manage their wildlife populations through the use of hunting seasons. Every state has hunting seasons for each type of wild game. A big game animal can be legally hunted only during its lawful hunting season, which has an opening date and a closing date. These dates can change from year to year.

Before actually hunting big game, every hunter needs proper training. People need to learn how to handle and shoot firearms and archery, and what their responsibilities are before, during, and after a hunt. It also takes planning, various outdoor skills, and knowledge about wildlife and environments to hunt big game.

CHAPTER 1

HUNTER EDUCATION

*H*unters need basic hunting skills and knowledge to go into the fields and woods to hunt wild animals. To be a good hunter takes ability, education, and patience. People must learn about their equipment and also how to shoot safely and accurately before they go hunting. The rifle is the most common type of firearm used to hunt large animals. Using the correct rifle and ammunition can make a hunt more enjoyable and increase the chance of success. Other options for weapons for hunting large wildlife are slug shotguns, muzzleloaders, handguns, and bows and arrows.

Buying a Firearm

The federal government controls all laws on buying firearms. The age of the firearm buyer is restricted. A parent or guardian must buy and register the firearm for young (underage) hunters. Each state controls the big game season and what type of weapons can be used and when. Some areas with flat land or farmland restrict hunters to a particular gun, which is usually a slug shotgun. Compared to those from a shotgun, bullets from rifles travel farther.

Rifles

Many big game hunters use scopes on their rifles. A scope is a small telescope that is mounted on top of a rifle. Hunters line up the crosshairs (guides) on the scope to aim accurately and be more precise with their shot. The magnification of a scope allows them to see an animal

The ability to place a rifle bullet at long distances on moving targets is a critical skill for big game hunters. A scope greatly improves the accuracy of shots taken at long distances.

better than with the unaided eye. A typical scope uses three times (3X) magnification. This means that an animal appears three times closer than it does without the scope.

Rifles are made to shoot a specific caliber of bullet. The larger the caliber is, the larger the bullet. The long, grooved barrel of a rifle increases the accuracy of the lead bullet as it is fired. The precision is due to the grooves that twist around inside the barrel. The grooves cause bullets to spin as they move through the barrel. The spin helps stabilize bullets, which increases their accuracy and allows them to travel great distances.

Many rifle models with different actions are available. The most common model for hunting large wildlife is a bolt action, in which the bolt is operated by hand. Many people think the bolt action is the most reliable and accurate rifle. Other popular rifle actions are pump, break, semiautomatic, and lever. Hunters often choose an action depending on where they will hunt. For example, high-powered rifles with bolt actions and good scopes are the choice in wide-open spaces for long distance shooting. Semiautomatic action rifles are typically used when fast-moving large animals are the target. Some hunters prefer lever or pump actions in wooded areas or if they walk while hunting.

Most states have laws that specify the minimum bullet caliber (diameter size) for big game hunting. The most common bullet sizes for rifles are the .30-30, .270, .30-06, and .308. Many big game hunters think that the .30-06 is the most versatile. These bullets travel a mile (1.6 km) or more and shoot accurately up to 300 yards (274 meters). The correct caliber for a rifle is stamped on its barrel.

Slug Shotguns, Muzzleloaders, and Handguns

A shotgun has a long, smooth barrel. For hunting big game, people use a shotgun that shoots slugs. Two popular slugs are the Sabot-type

Hundreds of different ammunitions are available to big game hunters. A common bullet is the 12-gauge shotgun slug. It is very accurate within 400 feet (120 meters).

and Foster-style. The Sabot-type has a long, slender shape. The Foster-style looks like a cup with twisted grooves on the outside. The grooves cause the bullet to spin, increasing its precision and distance. The 12-gauge slug shotgun is the most popular.

Some hunters like using muzzleloaders, also called black powder guns. These guns are loaded by putting black powder and a lead bullet into the muzzle, and pressing them down the barrel. The first shot must be a good one because reloading can take more than a minute. Hunters can choose muzzleloading shotguns and rifles. The most popular muzzleloading rifles for big game are 50 or 54 caliber. Many states have extended seasons for muzzleload hunting of big game.

Hunting large wildlife with a handgun or revolver takes great skill. Hunters must get close to an animal to make an accurate shot. Handguns that are single cartridge, five or six cartridges, and semiautomatic are available. Some handgun hunters mount a scope on the short barrel.

Bowhunting

Bowhunting, or shooting arrows with bows, is popular with many large wildlife hunters. People who shoot with a bow and arrow are called bowhunters or archers. It takes strength and special skills to bowhunt well. Hunters must build up their arm and shoulder muscles. Compared to hunters using rifles, archers need to get much closer to an animal to shoot because arrows do not travel as far as bullets. It is more difficult to accurately shoot large wildlife using a bow and arrow than with a firearm. In many states, bowhunters can hunt for a longer period of time than those who use firearms.

For big game, hunters use a compound bow or a recurve bow. The compound bow is the most popular. It is made up of a system of strings, wheels, and pulleys that reduces the amount of force needed to hold

Bowhunting requires precise placement of the arrow. Regular practice with a compound bow on targets greatly increases hunting success.

the bow while it is drawn and ready for release. Hunters like this bow because it increases their control while they wait for the right moment to shoot. The recurve bow curves back against its natural bend, which gives it great power when the arrow is released. Some hunters prefer the recurve bow because it is lighter and quieter to shoot than the compound bow.

The correct bow to use for big game depends on the strength and size of a hunter. Bows are rated in pounds to pull the string back. For example, a bow rated at 50 pounds (23 kg) requires 50 pounds (23 kg) of force (strength) to pull back the string to draw an arrow. The higher the force of a bow's strings, the faster and farther an arrow will travel.

Bowhunters who hunt large animals use the broadhead arrow. This arrow has two or more very sharp steel blades. A mechanical or expandable blade broadhead arrow expands when it hits something, which then exposes the blades. Many states have laws that specify the diameter and number of blades for broadhead arrows used for hunting big game. The key skill for a bowhunter to master is the exact placement of an arrow tipped with a broadhead.

Using Weapons Safely

Every state in the United States offers a hunter safety program. Most states require beginning hunters to take this class before their first hunt. The following are some of the important rules for the safe handling of weapons. Always assume a firearm is loaded and handle it carefully. Keep a firearm unloaded until ready to use it. When carrying a firearm, open the action, keep fingers away from the trigger, and keep the safety switch on. A safety can fail, so do not assume the safety will always work. Only point a weapon at the target and in a safe direction. Do not fire at only sound or movement or where hunters or other people might be. Never lean a firearm against a tree, rock, fence, or other object as it could fall and accidently fire. Because firearms make loud noise and release debris (fragments), a hunter should wear ear protectors and shooting glasses when he or she is on a shooting range or hunting. After using firearms, store them and the ammunition separately in safe and secure places.

Learning to Hunt

Beginning hunters need to learn how to use weapons safely and correctly, including handling, transporting, and carrying them while they are hunting. Beginning hunters often learn skills from family members or friends who pass the knowledge down through generations. Most states require beginning hunters to participate in an official state training program. A state's natural resources or conservation department typically offers hunter education classes. After completing and passing the course, beginning hunters can then buy a hunting license. Conservation and shooting clubs also offer hunter education classes and seminars before the start of each hunting season. Important classes are firearm safety, proper use of firearms, archery, regulations, and animal identification.

Whether using firearms or a bow and arrow, hunters need to be on the mark when shooting. They want to harvest an animal, not wound it or miss and scare it away. To become a good shot requires a lot of practice using a firearm or bow and arrow. Good hunters spend time at a target range shooting at practice targets to become familiar with their weapon. Most shooting ranges have outdoor and indoor targets. Beginning shooters aim at targets that are placed at close range. As they advance, they shoot at targets at longer ranges. Hunters can read books and go to Web sites for information about the safe use of weapons for hunting large animals. All hunters need to know the laws and responsibilities of hunting.

CHAPTER 2

HUNTER RESPONSIBILITY

*H*unters have the duty to protect, conserve, and improve the land and water resources of the nation. All states require hunters to follow laws that protect people, wildlife, and private property. Laws keep hunting safe and fair for all. Whether people use firearms, muzzleloaders, or archery, everybody has the same responsibilities when they are hunting.

Know the Laws

Hunters need to follow the federal and state laws that regulate the harvesting of big game animals. By law, hunters must shoot only specified weapons during an established season. They must harvest only the big game animals that are permissible. Most types of hunting have a season when it is legal to harvest each type of big game animal. Laws that

Every state and province requires a hunting license, and some require a wildlife stamp. Big game licenses are purchased annually.

manage the hunting of big game conserve wildlife by protecting the land from the animals' grazing to the point where it damages the vegetation and land cover. This overgrazing can harm the animals, too, by their losing their main source of food. These hunting laws guarantee the privilege to hunt. Authorities closely watch big game in all states. To enforce hunting laws, states run registration stations and require hunters to attach possession game tags on the harvested animals.

Most states require underage hunters to pass a hunting course and then obtain a hunting certificate. The department of natural resources certifies this hunter education course. The course covers firearms and hunting safety, transporting and carrying firearms, and the basics of shooting. Beginners also learn about hunting responsibility, being prepared, wildlife conservation, and identifying wildlife. To complete the course, students must pass a written test and show safe firearm handling skills. Then they receive a certificate.

For positive identification, most states require hunters to have their hunter's certificate or driver's license in their possession. In some states, hunters are expected to wear a backtag (a tag attached to the back of outer clothing) that displays their license number. The backtag displays a personal identification number. During the season, hunters must follow strict limits on the number of animals they can take. They must buy a license for each deer, elk, moose, bear, or wild boar (wild pig) that they want to hunt. Hunters can renew their hunting license to keep it current. Depending on the state, a license may be valid for specific days, specific months, or one year.

Hunting Ethics

Sometimes problems come up that are not covered by federal or state laws. Being a responsible hunter means making decisions and doing things the right way when no one is watching. Ethics is a personal decision beyond what the law requires. An ethical hunter is fair and respectful to animals, property, other hunters, and other people. Hunters follow a personal code, or a set of acceptable behaviors. A "hunter's code" is as important as hunting laws.

For example, some people think that they can hunt big game whenever they want. They might harvest wildlife outside of its season or during the season without following the regulations. Moreover, they might hunt without a license or game tags and harvest an animal. This illegal hunting is called poaching. When they are caught, the poachers will be fined. In most cases, they will lose their hunting privileges for years. They may also lose their hunting weapon, boats, and any motorized vehicle that was used when they poached.

Land Access

Hunters must know where it is legal to hunt wild animals. At all times, they must honor private property without trespassing. It is a crime to hunt on private land without permission when it is posted with "No Trespassing" or "No Hunting."

If they are allowed to hunt on private property, hunters need to be respectful of and responsible to landowners. Some of the rules to abide by are the following: Always ask the landowners for permission to hunt big game on their land, and thank them when the hunting is done. Treat private land, farm animals, crops, and equipment

Next to safety, the primary responsibility of a hunter is to honor private property. The hunter must follow all trespass laws and avoid illegal access.

carefully. After a successful hunt, it is a good idea to offer landowners some of the meat. If they do not want the meat, perhaps the hunter could return to help them work with crops or livestock, for example. By being respectful, hunters are often welcomed back each year by these landowners.

National and state forests are public lands. They are owned by all citizens. Big game hunters who are on public property have a duty to treat the land and campgrounds with care and keep the area clean by not littering. Furthermore, they can pick up litter that others have left behind.

Positive Public Image

It is important that responsible hunters show a positive image by being courteous and using common sense. Nonhunters and other hunters form opinions about big game hunters based on the big game hunters' actions. Hunters might meet other people enjoying the land and wildlife, such as hikers, bird watchers, and skiers. Responsible hunters do not want to frighten or offend people who are afraid of firearms or who do not approve of hunting. When they aren't hunting, these people keep firearms unloaded, in cases, and stored out of sight.

To be responsible, hunters must obey the laws involving big game. They need to know their rifle or archery equipment, how it works, and how to shoot accurately. Hunters must know where to aim and how to hit a deer, moose, elk, bear, or wild boar for a fast and humane kill. They need to keep improving their shooting skills with weapons so that they do not wound their target. They can do this by practicing, taking classes, and learning from other hunters. If someone in the hunting group wounds an animal, track, or help others to track, and recover the injured animal. When traveling from the hunting area, make sure to cover the harvested animal so it does not offend nonhunters.

Hunters become expert shooters by practicing in the off-season. The placement of a small bullet on a long-distance or moving target requires shooting skill.

Responsible hunters practice fair chase. They do not take unfair advantage of big game animals. For instance, hunters should not harvest an animal while it is eating illegal bait. Hunters are responsible for reading and following the state's definition of legal bait. Nor should they shoot an animal that is fenced in and cannot escape a hunter.

Hunters have a responsibility to make full use of the big game that they harvest. They should eat the meat. If they want to share harvested

Big game hunting is a privilege that provides exciting outdoor experiences. The sight of a bull (male) moose in its natural habitat is always a thrill.

big game, they need to check the state regulations before offering meat to others. Some states provide for successful hunters to donate their big game animal to a local food bank. Many hunters like to take photos of their harvested big game. It is a good idea to make sure the photos are tasteful so that nonhunters are not offended.

Other Hunters

Big game hunters are responsible to all other hunters. Being safe is of upmost importance. Hunters expect other hunters to obey hunting laws and to respect hunting areas and zones of fire. The area a hunter can shoot safely in is known as the zone of fire. When hunting alone, a hunter can shoot in any direction once the target and what is beyond it are clearly identified. However, a big game hunter must check that other hunters are not sharing the same hunting area.

When hunting in groups, it is important that each hunter knows exactly where he or she can shoot and not put other partners in danger. Hunting partners need to talk to set up the zone of fire for each other before they begin to shoot.

Even when partners have established their range of fire, more than one hunter might shoot at and harvest the same animal. Then they need to make a responsible decision as to who tags the big game. One decision could be that the youngest hunter gets the animal. Another decision might be that they agree to share the meat.

Supporting Wildlife

By law, big game hunters pay annual license and tag fees for the animals they want to hunt. Hunters also pay state and local taxes on hunting equipment. Funding of wildlife programs comes from these fees and taxes. Many types of wildlife, including wildlife that is not hunted, benefit from these management programs. Every year, hunting organizations across the nation raise millions of dollars for restoring or improving animal habitats and wildlife research and education.

Hunters need to know and promote wildlife conservation programs that guarantee stable wildlife populations for both hunters and non-hunters to enjoy. If an animal population gets too small and is in danger of becoming extinct, the federal or state government declares it endangered. It is illegal to hunt endangered animals. One of the main reasons that animal populations decline is because people use the animal's habitat. Local and national hunting associations work together with other conservation organizations to protect wildlife. They may do this by setting aside large pieces of wild land to conserve habitats. When hunters follow hunting seasons and limits, they are respecting conservation efforts. They leave enough members of an animal population to guarantee a future stable population.

On the other hand, if a wildlife population gets too large, the animals cannot find enough food or water. They might eat most or all of certain plants in an area, which ruins the plant environment. A plant environment that is overgrazed will lead to the animal population starving, moving to a new area, or becoming extinct. If starving, the animals might get sick and infect other wild animals with disease. Hunters help by thinning or reducing deer, wild boars, or other large animals to avoid overpopulating an area.

CHAPTER 3

PLANNING THE HUNT

Planning ahead is key to a safe and successful hunt. Big game hunters need to line up a place to hunt and observe and study the animals in their environment. They need to learn the animal's habitat and behavior. They use this knowledge, along with other skills, such as marksmanship, to help them hunt. Hunters also need to prepare in other ways.

Finding a Place to Hunt

Hunters are responsible for finding a place to hunt big game. They may need to get reservations and permits to hunt on public lands and wildlife management areas. Wildlife managers and conservation officers can provide this information. These officials might know of farmers or ranchers who want hunters to reduce their big game population. Hunters can check the local assessor's office or county Web sites to find owners who welcome hunters. Sometimes, members of a hunting group know of a private or public place. National forests are often open to big game hunters. The United States Forest Service administers these large blocks of public land.

Hunters must contact a landowner and ask permission to hunt on private land for a particular type of big game. Summer is the best time to contact landowners. Hunters should scout the land to get to know it and the wildlife living there. Studying the land with topographic and aerial maps increases a hunter's knowledge of where animals live.

Learning Animal Habitats and Behavior

All big game animals live where their plant food is available, usually in forests and on mountains, and along streams and lakes. Big game animals gather much information through their keen senses of smell and hearing. Deer, for example, can detect a person who is many blocks away by smelling. Most game animals do not travel far to find food and water. However, moose, elk, and bears will go long distances to search for food if necessary. These large animals require a lot of food to stay healthy. When hunters can find where animals feed, their success of harvesting big game increases greatly.

Deer, Moose, and Elk

Deer, moose, and elk are members of the deer family. They have cloven hoofs of two parts, antlers that shed every year, and brown coats that blend in with their surroundings. Their diet is grass, low-growing plants such as clover, tree leaves, buds, and acorns. They also feed on almost any farm crop.

White-tailed deer rate as the number one big game animal in North America. They are found in all fifty states and much of Canada.

The successful big game hunter studies the wild animal's habits and habitats prior to the actual hunt. Knowing these characteristics of a white-tailed buck (male) deer increases the likelihood of a harvest.

Most live along forest and field edges and brushy, low woodlands. Mule deer inhabit the western third of North America in brushy areas, forests, desert shrubs, and rock uplands. Deer often outsmart hunters with their amazing ability to disappear. When sensing danger, deer quickly find an escape path or a patch of cover. Fast runners, deer can reach 35 to 40 miles (56 to 64 km) per hour for short distances and easily jump an obstacle 8 feet (2.5 m) high. They are also strong swimmers. Mule deer have better vision than white-tailed deer. Of the more than two dozen varieties of white-tailed deer in North America, the largest is the northern white-tailed, which weighs up to 250 pounds (113 kg). Mule deer have large rabbitlike ears. The Rocky Mountain mule deer is the largest of the seven varieties, weighing up to 400 pounds (181 kg).

Moose inhabit the northern United States and most of Canada. They live in thick forests near shallow water. The lakes, marshes, and swamps provide a source of food. Like deer, moose are excellent swimmers and can run fast, up to 30 miles (48 km) per hour. They have poorer sight than deer. Moose usually live by themselves. Elk are somewhat smaller than moose. A large male moose weighs 1,400 pounds (635 kg), and a large elk is about 1,100 pounds (499 kg). Although elk prefer grassy meadows, they will go to higher land or deep into a forest if danger approaches. Sometimes, large herds, or groups, will move up to 100 miles (161 km) to find food. Elk trot long distances at 15 to 20 miles (24 to 32 km) per hour, with bursts of speed of 35 miles (56 km) per hour.

Bears and Wild Boars

Bears are intelligent game animals. Although they have poor eyesight, they have excellent senses of smell and hearing. Black bears are the most hunted variety of bear in much of the United States, but they are not common in the Midwest and Texas. They inhabit forests, swamps, and mountains. Like members of the deer family, bears eat grasses and crops. They also eat berries, fruits, nuts, insects, small animals, and fish.

Black bears live throughout much of the United States. Controlled hunting seasons have guaranteed a stable bear population.

Bears are nimble, able to climb a tree in seconds, and can run 25 miles (40 km) per hour for short distances. Standing 5 to 6 feet (1.5 to 1.8 m) tall, a male black bear weighs 200 to 400 or more pounds (91 to 181 kg or more).

Wild boars are hunted with liberal limits and seasons. This animal is considered a nuisance and requires hunting to control its population growth.

Like bears, wild pigs are intelligent, and they eat the same diet. Wild boars also dig up the ground to find roots to eat. The largest populations of wild boars live in the Appalachian Mountains and in the southern United States. The most hunted wild pig is the razorback.

Big game hunters appreciate a new snowfall for scouting. The snow allows the hunter to determine how many and where the animals are living prior to the actual hunt. These are deer tracks.

Male wild pigs weigh up to 400 pounds (181 kg) or more. They have two large tusks (long, pointed teeth) that project from the lower jaw. They use these to dig for food or as weapons.

Scouting for Big Game

Big game hunters should scout their hunting area in advance of the season. If they are unfamiliar with an area, they may want to scout with an experienced hunter. By scouting, hunters become familiar with the land

Tracks of a bear are often the only sign indicating where the animal is living. Bears are usually nocturnal (active at night), so skillful observation of tracks and scat is critical for success.

and can identify where to find the wildlife they want. Hunters look for changes in the habitat or population size. In particular, severe weather or shortages of food could cause big game populations to move to a new area.

Sometimes, spotting big game is difficult. Hunters can look for other animal signs, such as game trails that go from cover (bedding or hiding place) to food or water. Deer, for instance, typically use the same trails. Hunters can examine animal tracks in the soil or snow. Large amounts of scat (animal droppings) in an area means the animals have been eating or bedding there. Experienced hunters know what animals have been eating by looking at the nipped ends of grasses, twigs, or crops. Each type of big game animal has its own chew marks. Male deer during breeding season leave scrapes on the ground and rubs on trees. These marks identify the location of the animals. Some hunters place camcorders in potential hunting areas to record wildlife movements. They watch the photography to determine the behavior of the animals and how many are in the area.

Safety Tips

Being in good physical condition is important for a person so that he or she has an enjoyable hunt. Sometimes, hunters walk long distances and carry heavy equipment. If they are not in good shape, hunters should start a regular exercise program at least two months before their planned hunt. An exercise program includes aerobic exercise, also called cardio or endurance activity. Aerobic exercise is physical activity that uses large muscle groups and increases the heart rate for a period of time. Examples include walking briskly, jogging, hiking, skiing, biking, or swimming laps. Sports such as basketball and football are also aerobic exercise.

Survival and First Aid Kits

For emergencies, every hunter should carry a survival kit when scouting and hunting. Sporting stores sell survival packs. Hunters can make their own pack. A survival kit should contain a map of the area, a knife, a flashlight with working batteries, extra water and food, a compass, a whistle, and materials to start a fire, including waterproof matches. A large, thick garbage bag can provide the hunter with protection from cold, wind, snow, or rain. In addition, hunters should always bring a first aid kit. The type of first aid kit depends on the land, climate, and distance from a vehicle or cabin. Most kits contain bandages, tape, small scissors, aspirin or non-aspirin pain relievers, tweezers, cotton swabs, and a first aid handbook. Sun-blocking lotion and personal medicines should also go in a first aid kit. Taking a first aid course is a good objective for anyone who wishes to hunt.

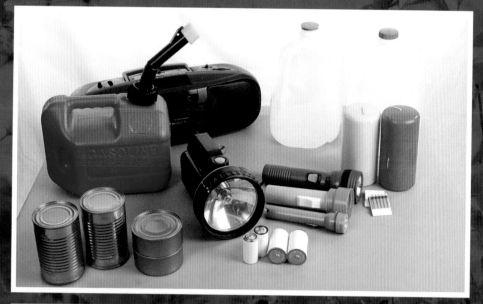

Every hunter must think before the hunt about what items would be necessary if an emergency occurs. Every hunt is different because of the distance and type of wild land being covered.

Hunters need to plan for the unexpected and know how to survive in an emergency situation. They should always tell someone where they are going and when they expect to return, and never scout or hunt alone. Knowing how to build a fire and signal for help are necessary outdoor skills.

What to Bring

When scouting and hunting, people bring their survival and first aid kits and other useful items. Binoculars help them look for big game and identify legal big game animals. Experienced hunters carry a compass or use a global positioning system (GPS). They bring a cell phone for emergency calls.

Many states require hunters to wear blaze orange clothing so that other hunters can see them. Hunters might wear blaze orange vests and hats, even if they are not required by law to do so. Most bowhunters also wear camouflage clothing, which helps to keep animals from seeing them in the woods. In cold weather, hunters dress warmly and in layers, and wear hiking boots made of leather or rubber.

Hunters often bring sleeping bags to stay warm if they plan to be long distances from a vehicle. They might bring tents to provide shelter from wind and rain. Weather can change quickly and make hunting dangerous.

CHAPTER 4

HUNTING METHODS

*E*very hunting trip is different. Hunters need to know multiple ways to help make their hunt successful. The method used for a particular hunt depends on many factors, such as the number of people in the hunting group, the land, weather, and type of weapon. Hunters must also consider wind direction and how close they will be to buildings and nonhunters.

Stand Hunting

Hunting from a tree stand is a popular way to pursue game. Hunters sit in stands above trees and brush to see into forest, bushes, or grass. They can look farther than if they were on the ground. A stand must offer a clear field of vision to shoot into. Stand hunting is used for any big game, particularly white-tailed deer and bear. This method is adaptable to both firearms and archery.

A common still hunting technique is to hunt from a permanent stand. Hunters must make sure that permission from the landowner is obtained before building a hunting stand.

Although a stand can be a sturdy tree branch, most hunters use an elevated platform that is made in a tree or pulled up into a tree. The stand attaches to a limb or the trunk of a tree. Most stands hold one person. Big game should not be able to see a hunter in a stand.

Stand hunting can take some preparation time unless hunters know an area well. A few weeks before the season, hunters should carefully scout the land to find feeding, drinking, or bedding areas of the big game they want. After determining a place with many signs of wildlife activity, hunters select a tree and make their stand. Cautious animals often stay away from a new stand location for some time. During the season, hunters sit and wait in their stand for big game to pass by. Hunters might sit for many hours. Stand hunting works best early, often before sunrise, or late in the day. During these times animals move between feeding and resting places.

The wind is another important factor when choosing a site for a tree stand. Hunters build their tree stand downwind. This means that the wind is in the faces of hunters, as they look at the area most likely to be used by the hunted animals. Most hunters have alternative stands for different wind conditions. Some use scent blockers to keep animals from smelling them. Animals will change their patterns of movement if an unusual scent, noise, or movement arises.

Still or Stationary Hunting

Still or stationary hunting means silent hunting. Still hunters sneak through the woods to get close to big game. They move upward and into the wind backward and stop often so that they can surprise an animal without it seeing them. By slowly moving, still hunters keep alert for sights, sounds, or smells that mean big game is nearby. Animals watch for movement and sounds to signal danger, so they are less likely to spot hunters who are silent and stepping carefully. Still hunting works

Hunters who still hunt increase their chance of success by using camouflage clothing and equipment. Camouflage gives the hunter an advantage when moving slowly and stalking into close range of a wild animal.

best when big game is bedded down or not active, typically during the middle of the day.

The way people still hunt is to take unhurried steps and stop. They slowly move only their head and eyes to search the area for an animal, and repeat. Usually, big game hunters walk silently about five minutes, and then wait and look in all directions for about five minutes. The best places to still hunt are in areas where animals live or frequent, like watering holes. Another place for still hunting is if there is a good food source nearby, such as a stand of oak trees with acorns or high-bush cranberries.

All types of weapons can be used when still hunting. Although stationary hunting can be done any place, it is best in thick woods and in shade. Animals are likely to notice sun glare off of the face and clothing in sunlight. No preparation is needed to still hunt, although a basic idea of where animals live is important. Moose hunters, for instance, can check the banks of streams for game trails leading to the water. People need to determine if the weather and wind are correct to still hunt. To keep animals from seeing them, hunters should not walk across open areas. Usually still hunting is done by one person, but it works well with two people. The second hunter follows far behind the first.

Baiting

In some states, baiting is a legal way to attract big game to a place for stand hunting. This method is very effective for white-tailed deer, bear, or wild boar. Baiting requires advance planning. Every day, hunters must put out food in an area in advance of the season. Good bait for deer is dried corn. Bears like candy, honey, cookies, and other sweets. Wild pigs eat any type of food. Over time, hunters note where big game enters the baiting place to feed. They will also see tracks of the animal. Hunters then build their tree stand near the feeding area and wait for the big game to come and feed. It is important to check what the law allows for baiting. For example, states typically restrict who can bait, when baiting is allowed, and the amount of food placed at feeding sites. Usually, bait must be a certain distance from trails, roads, or campsites used by the public.

Stalking or Walking Hunt

Like still hunting, stalking requires excellent hunting skills. Hunters sneak up on big game without being detected. Although it is difficult to creep up within shooting range, experienced hunters can get less than 100 feet (30 m) from an animal. To stalk, hunters follow a game trail to a bedded or feeding animal. Another method they use is to spot big game on a hill or mountainside and move toward it slowly. Bowhunters and rifle hunters stalk.

Hunters need to stay behind land formations, trees, and brush until they are close enough to shoot an animal. A walking hunt is difficult in thick woods because hunters cannot see their big game. Stalkers stay behind hills, trees, brush, tall crops or grass, or fencing so that an animal cannot see them. When hunting in open, flat land, stalkers often carry a clump of brush or weeds as cover. Stalking works well to hunt elk and black bears on mountainsides. Mule deer on high hills or in mountainous areas are also hunted in this way.

Most stalkers use binoculars to spot big game. Seeing an animal from a distance allows them to plan how and what path they will take to stalk. After seeing an animal, hunters watch it closely for a few minutes. They try to determine whether it will stay in the same place. After stalking, an animal that is still feeding or lying down is usually close enough for a shot.

A walking hunt requires basic knowledge of the land and animal habitats. This method works well any time during the season. It does not require much advance preparation. An important skill that stalkers need is to accurately predict the weather. They must determine wind direction so that they can move upwind (wind in the face) without the animal smelling or hearing them. Experienced stalkers move only when an animal faces away from them or has its head down to feed or drink. They make sure that sunlight does not reflect off their gun or scope.

Stalking or group drives are common methods used to hunt wary mule deer bucks in forested areas. The white-tailed deer can also be hunted in wooded areas by using these methods.

When they get close to their animal, they move as silently as possible until a successful shot can be made.

Drive or Group Hunting

Sometimes, hunters use driving as a way to push or move animals out of their cover. To drive hunt, hunters line up and walk through woods or fields to move animals toward other hunters waiting nearby. This method is typically used by larger groups to hunt white-tailed deer or elk. Any firearm can be used for drives. However, group hunting is most effective with rifles because the animals are moving fast and sometimes are a long distance away. Animals responding to a drive are often moving too quickly for archers to make accurate shots. Some states allow dogs to be used as drivers when hunting for big game.

Depending on the situation, group hunting can work with a dozen or more hunters, but usually it is best with two to six people. Before the drive begins, people known as posters quietly move to positions at the end of the cover and stand still. Drivers spread out across the woods or fields. Usually, more drivers are needed than standers.

Because group hunting can be dangerous, safety rules are a priority. Beginners need to stay within arm's reach of experienced hunters. Another safety rule is that hunters must always know the positions of drivers and posters. No one should shoot when a hunter might be in the line of fire. Furthermore, all hunters must wear blaze orange clothing.

CHAPTER 5

AFTER THE HUNT

*A*fter harvesting a wild animal, hunters do several things for a successful completion of the hunt. First, they retrieve it and dress the animal in the forest or field. After transporting it to camp or home, the animal is skinned and butchered. The meat is cut into smaller sections and is then ready to be cooked and eaten. Hunters should thank the other hunters and private landowners who helped in the harvest.

Tracking

After hunters shoot at an animal, they determine if it was killed, wounded, or missed. Wounded big game often run some distance and must be tracked. They might run more than 100 yards (91 m) even when they are hit in the heart-lung area. Wounded large animals can be difficult to find because they may not show that they have been hit. If an animal is not seriously wounded, hunters usually wait thirty to sixty minutes before tracking it. During this waiting time, the animal will weaken from blood loss and lie down. However, during rain or snow, hunters often track wounded wildlife immediately so the tracks do not disappear.

To track, hunters note where the big game was hit. They mark the spot with a piece of clothing or colored survey tape, or use a landmark such as a tree or rock. Then they quickly and quietly follow the blood trail. If hunters cannot see blood, they will walk in widening circles, looking for signs of the wounded animal at the spot where the animal was shot. Signs of a shot might be drops of blood, hair, fragments of bone, or unusual tracks of the animal. Tracking is easiest with two or more hunters. If they cannot find the animal, hunters return to their starting point and try a second time.

Field Dressing and Transporting

Once big game is harvested, hunters must get to their animal. They carefully approach a shot animal from behind. A shot that is well placed can kill an animal instantly. If the shot is not well-aimed, the animal might be stunned and could seriously harm a hunter by lashing out with its sharp hoofs, antlers, claws, or tusks. Hunters must keep their weapon ready for a second shot as they approach a downed animal.

Next is field dressing, or butchering. This step is key to cool the animal quickly, which preserves the meat. Wearing latex gloves when available, hunters cut open the body cavity with a sharp knife. They remove the windpipe, stomach, intestines, and all other organs. Some people wipe out the cavity with dry grass or with a cloth.

Hunters must follow the regulations of the state and license tag their harvested animal. Tagging means to punch the day and month of the kill on a tag and attach it to the animal. If allowed by law, hunters

This hunter in a tree stand is about to harvest a big game animal. After the harvest, she will need to field dress, tag, and haul the animal out of the woods.

prefer to attach the tag after field dressing and dragging, so that the tag does not get ripped off during this process. Hunters may need to transport the animal to a registration and checking station to receive a permanent possession tag.

To transport the harvested animal home or to a station, hunters tie rope around the neck or antlers, and wrap the rope around the animal's muzzle or snout. Then they haul, usually by dragging, the animal out of the woods or brush. Often more than one hunter pulls because a harvested big game animal typically weighs more than 100 pounds (45 kg). Dragging on snow usually does little damage to the animal's fur.

Dragging on bare ground can ruin the hide, so hunters must carefully pull or carry the animal out of the woods. Hunters hoist the harvested animal on top of their vehicle or into a trailer, cover it with a tarp, and tie the animal down.

Making Use of Big Game

Some hunters bring the carcass (harvested animal) to professional butchers who prepare the meat for eating. If hunters butcher their animal, they must follow safe methods. To begin the process, they remove the hide from the carcass right away. Next, they cut off the neck, saw the animal in half, and cut the halves into smaller sections of steaks and roasts. Many hunters age their big game meat at 42 degrees Fahrenheit (5.5 degrees Celsius) because it becomes tender and tastes better. Aging is often done by keeping the large sections cool and dry for a week or more. One way to do this is to wrap the large sections in a cotton sack and hang them in a cool garage or shed. After aging, the meat is ready to be cut into smaller pieces for cooking or freezing.

Big game meat is tasty and nutritious! Some hunters enjoy learning how to cook wild meat. It is prepared in many healthy ways, such as in soups, stews, stir-frys, and as jerky, steaks, or roasts. Big game meat is lean and lower in fat and calories than beef. If a wild boar is harvested, some people roast the entire carcass on a spit and invite friends over for a banquet.

To keep the memory of a good hunt, hunters might take photographs or videos of their harvest to share with family, friends, and other hunters. They can take photos in the woods or field, or at home. Some hunters use the antlers of their big game as coat racks or in art work. They might mount the antlers on a wall as a display.

Some hunters want the head of their big game as a trophy. Taxidermists are professionals who mount big game trophies. They start

Taxidermy is the preservation of the head or body of a successfully hunted wild animal. The mounts provide years of memories and discussion for many big game hunters.

by covering a premade foam model of the animal with special glue. Then they carefully stretch and fit the tanned hide of the big game on the model and add glass eyes. After the glue dries, the trophy is ready to mount on a wall.

47

Big Game Hides

Some hunters tan their big game hides to use as rugs or blankets, or to make warm clothing. Another use is to hang them above a fireplace or on a wall. Tanning is not difficult to do, but it takes time. Instead of tanning at home, many hunters take their hides to taxidermists. If hunters cannot use their hides, they can donate them at drop-off sites. Some states have Hides-for-Habitat programs. Hunters donate deer hides to these programs. The hides are sold, and the money goes for habitat projects throughout the state, wildlife research, and educational programs for children and teens. The Elks, a national organization, has an annual drive to collect deer, elk, and other animal hides to benefit disabled war veterans. The hides are sold, and the money is donated to veteran's hospitals. Alternatively, veterans can use the hides for craft kits to make purses, wallets, moccasins, gloves, and clothes.

Bear hunters commonly have the hide tanned by a professional taxidermist. The soft bear fur makes a warm and beautiful blanket or rug.

Preparing for the Next Hunt

Preparation for the next hunt begins as soon as hunters come home. They clean their weapon and other equipment and wash dirty clothes. They sharpen and oil their knives, and take batteries out of headlights and flashlights. Anything used in hunting that is broken should be replaced. If hunting clothing or equipment is needed, hunters watch for off-season sales to buy them. All items are then packed for the next hunt.

Many hunters keep a journal of their hunt, making notes of everything interesting that happened. They can keep a journal by hand or in an electronic document. They also need to remember to map where they hunted. They can go to the Web site of the state nature resources department or to Google Earth to make a map, or mark a paper map.

Hunters can learn more about hunting and big game in numerous ways. Many join local hunting and sporting clubs. They can take classes at the clubs and share information on local big game populations and hunting. They can research hunting techniques and big game through books, magazines, and the Internet.

Many state and national organizations offer teen hunter programs. These events are often at local sporting clubs and schools. Some events test hunter knowledge and shooting and other skills. The National Rifle Association holds the Youth Hunter Education Challenge program. Teen hunters compete in outdoor weapon shooting of game animal

The ability to read and understand topographical maps is an important skill for big game hunters. The maps provide an accurate placement of past hunts and can be used to plan future hunts.

targets under real field conditions. They can also take a written test about hunting ethics and safety issues. The National 4-H Organization offers a Shooting Sports program. Some nature centers and community education programs provide courses in survival skills and compass orientation. First aid courses are available through local American Red Cross chapters.

Hunters might not harvest an animal during every hunt. Each hunt, however, provides hunters with a healthy outdoor experience and practice. They improve their knowledge of safety precautions and hunting skills, and big game habitat and behavior. Good hunters stay up to date with laws and regulations because these can change. Big game hunting provides challenging and exciting memories that will last a lifetime. Moreover, it allows hunters the chance for delicious meals of big game meat.

aerial Carried out from the air, particularly using aircraft, as in aerial photography of a region.

ammunition Bullets and gun powder used in firearms.

antlers Bony structures that quickly develop from bone pads or lumps on the head of a male deer, moose, or elk. Antlers are shed after the breeding season.

archery The skill of shooting with a bow and arrow.

bait The food used to lure wild game to within shooting range.

barrel The steel tube of a rifle.

bedding area The sleeping area of an animal.

black powder An explosive mixture used as a propellant in muzzleloaders.

butcher To process an animal's meat into usable sizes.

caliber The inside diameter of the barrel of a rifle or the diameter of a bullet.

camouflage Anything that conceals a person or equipment by making it appear to be part of the natural surroundings.

conservation Protection and preservation of nature.

endangered In danger of becoming extinct.

extinct No longer existing.

field dressing Preparing a recently harvested animal so that its body temperature lowers and the meat stays fresh.

game Wild animals hunted for food or sport.

global positioning system (GPS) Handheld computer that can calculate an exact position using a global positioning satellite.

habitat The area or environment where an animal lives.

harvest The act of shooting and recovering an animal.

hide The skin of an animal.

illegal Against the law.

marksmanship The ability to shoot skillfully at a target or mark.

muzzle The open end of a gun barrel.

poach To take game in a forbidden area or game that is illegal to take.

safety A device on a firearm that keeps it from being fired.

scope A small telescope on a rifle barrel.

season Length of time to hunt specific game.

slug A lead bullet used in shotguns.

stand hunting A type of hunting in which a hunter uses a tree stand or an elevated platform to wait for the game to appear.

target Something that is aimed and shot at with firearms or bow and arrow.

topographic Relating to the accurate representation of the physical features of an area.

track To follow an animal.

trespass To unlawfully enter a person's property.

American Deer & Wildlife Alliance

12885 Research Boulevard, Suite 108A

Austin, TX 78750

(877) 331-8607

Web site: http://www.deerwildlifealliance.org

The American Deer & Wildlife Alliance serves as a national voice for organizations, companies, and professionals within the wildlife industries for the promotion and advancement of deer and other wildlife.

Canadian Parks and Wilderness Society

506-250 City Centre Avenue

Ottawa, ON K1R 6K7

Canada

(800) 333-9453

Web site: http://www.cpaws.org

This organization focuses on protecting many important areas of Canada's wilderness.

Canadian Shooting Sports Association

7 Director Court, Unit #106

Vaughan, ON L4L 4S5

Canada

(888) 873-4339

Web site: http://www.cdnshootingsports.org

The Canadian Shooting Sports Association promotes shooting sports, including hunting and archery. It supports and sponsors competitions and youth programs, and conducts training classes.

International Hunter Education Association

2727 West 92nd Avenue, Suite 103

Federal Heights, CO 80260

(303) 430-7233

Web site: http://www.ihea.com

The International Hunter Education Association is the professional association for state and provincial wildlife conservation agencies, and the instructors who teach hunter education in North America.

National Bowhunter Education Foundation

P.O. Box 180757

Fort Smith, AR 72918

(479) 649-9036

Web site: http://www.nbef.org

This organization provides bowhunting education and classes across the United States.

National Rifle Association of America

11250 Waples Mill Road

Fairfax, VA 22030

(800) 672-3888

Web site: http://www.nra.org

The National Rifle Association of America provides firearm education throughout the world.

National Shooting Sports Foundation

Flintlock Ridge Office Center

11 Mile Hill Road

Newtown, CT 06470-2359

(203) 426-1320

Web site: http://www.nssf.org

The mission of the National Shooting Sports Foundation is to promote, protect, and preserve hunting and the shooting sports.

National Wildlife Federation

11100 Wildlife Center Drive

Reston, VA 20190-5362

(800) 822-9919

Web site: http://www.nwf.org

The National Wildlife Federation works to protect and restore wildlife habitats.

Theodore Roosevelt Conservation Partnership

555 Eleventh Street NW, 6th Floor

Washington, DC 20004

(202) 654-4600

Web site: http://www.trcp.org/about.html

The Theodore Roosevelt Conservation Partnership works to preserve the traditions of hunting and fishing.

U.S. Fish and Wildlife Service

1849 C Street NW

Washington, DC 20240

(800) 344-9453

Web site: http://www.fws.gov

This government agency is dedicated to the conservation, protection, and enhancement of wildlife and plants and their habitats. Its primary responsibility is management of these important natural resources for the American public.

U.S. Forest Service

Attn: Office of Communication
Mailstop: 1111
1400 Independence Avenue SW
Washington, DC 20250-1111
(800) 832-1355
Web site: http://www.fs.fed.us
An agency of the U.S. Department of Agriculture, the Forest Service manages
the millions of acres of public lands in national forests and grasslands.

U.S. Sportsmen's Alliance

801 Kingsmill Parkway
Columbus, OH 43229
(614) 888-4868
Web site: http://www.ussportsmen.org
The U.S. Sportsmen's Alliance works to protect and advance the rights of
hunters and scientific wildlife management professionals.

Web Sites

Due to the changing nature of Internet links, Rosen Publishing has developed
an online list of Web sites related to the subject of this book. This site is
updated regularly. Please use this link to access the list:

http://www.rosenlinks.com/hunt/bgh

Alsheimer, Charles J. *Strategies for Whitetails*. Iola, WI: Krause
    Publications, 2006.

Andrews, Harris, and James A. Smith. *The Pocket Field Dressing Guide: The
    Complete Guide to Dressing Game*. Accokeek, MD: Stoeger Publishing
    Company, 2007.

Furtman, Michael. *Deer Tails & Trails: The Complete Book of Everything
    Whitetail*. Minocqua, WI: Willow Creek Press, 2006.

Geist, Valerius. *Moose: Behavior, Ecology, Conservation*. McGregor, MN:
    Voyageur Press, 2005.

Gross, W. H. *Young Beginner's Guide to Shooting and Archery: Tips for Gun
    and Bow*. Minneapolis, MN: Creative Publishing international, 2009.

Houston, Jay. *Elk Hunting 101: A Pocketbook Guide to Elk Hunting*. Lake
    Saint Louis, MO: Creek Publishers, 2004.

Lauber, Lon E. *Bowhunter's Guide to Accurate Shooting*. Minneapolis, MN:
    Creative Publishing international, 2005.

Lewis, Gary. *Complete Guide to Hunting: Basic Techniques for Gun and Bow
    Hunters*. Minneapolis, MN: Creative Publishing international, 2008.

Lewis, Gary, and Lee Van Tassel. *Black Bear Hunting: Expert Strategies for
    Success*. Minneapolis, MN: Creative Publishing international, 2007.

Sorrells, Brian J. *Beginner's Guide to Traditional Archery*. Mechanicsburg, PA:
    Stackpole Books, 2004.

Triplett, Todd. *The Complete Book of Wild Boar Hunting: Tips and Tactics
    That Will Work Anywhere*. Guilford, CT: The Lyons Press, 2004.

BIBLIOGRAPHY

Baird, Joel Banner. "Hunters as Environmental Stewards." November 29, 2009. Retrieved January 2, 2010 (http://www.burlingtonfreepress.com/article/20091129/LIVING09/91125050/Hunters-as-environmental-stewards).

Boddington, Craig. *Fair Chase in North America*. Missoula, MT: Boone & Crockett Club, 2004.

Boddington, Craig. *The Perfect Shot, North America: Shot Placement for North American Big Game*. Huntington Beach, CA: Safari Press, 2006.

Coor, Sam. "Hunters with Drive." *Duluth News Tribune,* November 22, 2009, pp. E1, E3.

Cord Communications. *The Experts' Book of Big Game Hunting in North America*. New York, NY: Cord Communications Corporation, 1976.

Creative Publishing editors. *Dressing and Cooking Wild Game.* Minneapolis, MN: Creative Publishing international, 2000.

Creative Publishing editors. *Hunting in North America*. Minneapolis, MN: Creative Publishing international, 2000.

Farrell, Sean Patrick. "The Urban Deerslayer." *New York Times*, November 24, 2009. Retrieved November 25, 2009 (http://www.nytimes.com/2009/11/25/dining/25hunt.html).

Fischl, Josef, and Leonard Lee Rue, III. *After Your Deer Is Down: The Care and Handling of Big Game*. Tulsa, OK: Winchester Press, 1981.

Kalthoff, Ken. "Hunters to Bring Not-So-Little Piggies to Market." January 20, 2010. Retrieved January 21, 2010 (http://www.nbcdfw.com/news/local-beat/Wild-Hogs-Run-Rampant-in-Texas-82219607.html.)

Lewis, Gary. *The Complete Guide to Hunting*. Minneapolis, MN: Creative Publishing international, 1999.

Lund, Duane R. *A Beginner's Guide to Hunting and Trapping Secrets*. Cambridge, MN: Adventure Publications, 1988.

Maas, David R. *North American Game Animals*. Minnetonka, MN: Cy Decosse, 1995.

Meili, Launi. *Rifle: Steps to Success*. Champaign, IL: Human Kinetics, 2008.

National Shooting Sports Foundation. *The Ethical Hunter*, pamphlet, 2006.

National Shooting Sports Foundation. *Firearms Safety Depends on You*, pamphlet, 2006.

National Shooting Sports Foundation. *The Hunter and Conservation*, booklet, 2006.

O'Connor, Jack. *The Art of Hunting Big Game in North America*. New York, NY: Outdoor Life, 1967.

Outdoor Empire Publishing. *Minnesota Firearms Safety Hunter Education, Student Manual*. Seattle, WA: Outdoor Empire Publishing, 2001.

Peterson, David H. (Hunter Education Instructor, Two Harbors, MN) in discussion with the author, January 2010.

INDEX

A

aerobic exercise, 32
aging meat, 46
American Red Cross, 52
animal overpopulation, 6, 23, 24

B

backtags, 17
baiting, 20, 39
bears, 4, 17, 19, 25, 27–29, 35, 39, 40
big game hides, uses for, 5, 49
big game meat, 4–5, 19, 20–22, 43, 46, 52
binoculars, 34, 40
blaze orange clothing, 34, 42
bowhunting and archery, 6, 11–13, 14, 34, 35, 40
broadhead arrow, 12–13
butchering, 43, 46

C

compound bow, 11–12

D

deer, 4, 17, 19, 23, 25–28, 32, 35, 39, 40, 42

E

elk, 4, 17, 19, 25, 27, 40, 42
endangered and extinct species, 6, 23

F

fair chase, 20
fees, 22–23
field dressing, 43, 44, 45
firearms, 6, 13, 14, 15, 16, 19, 35, 40, 42
  buying, 7–8
  types of, 8–11

first aid kits, 33, 34
4-H Shooting Sports program, 52

G

game tags, 16, 44
global positioning system (GPS), 34
group hunting, 42

H

handguns, 11
hunter's journal, 50
hunting
  education and training, 6, 7, 13–14, 16–17, 19, 50–52
  equipment, 22, 34, 50
  ethics, 17, 19–20
  laws, 6, 13, 14, 15–18, 19, 52
  safety, 13–14, 22, 32–33, 42

L

land access, 18–19, 24–25
licenses, 6, 14, 22

M

mapping, 25, 50, 52
moose, 4, 17, 19, 25, 27, 39
muzzleloaders, 11, 15

N

National Rifle Association, 52

P

poaching, 17
preparing for future hunts, 50–51

About the Author

Judy Monroe Peterson is married to an avid hunter who has more than fifty years of hunting experience. She has earned two master's degrees and is the author of more than fifty educational books for young people. Currently, she is a writer and editor of K–12 and post–high school curriculum materials on a variety of subjects, including biology, life science, and the environment.

About the Consultant

Benjamin Cowan has over twenty years of both big game and small game hunting experience. In addition to being an avid hunter, Mr. Cowan is also a member of many conservation organizations. He currently resides in west Tennessee.

Photo Credits

Cover, pp. 1, 3 © www.istockphoto.com/Bruce MacQueen; p. 5 Jupiterimages/Comstock Images/Getty Images; pp. 7, 15, 24, 35, 43 (silhouettes) © www.istockphoto.com/Michael Olson and Hemera/Thinkstock; pp. 8, 10, 12, 21, 26, 28, 33, 36, 41 Shutterstock.com; pp. 16, 38, 48–49 © AP Images; p. 18 William Thomas Cain/Getty Images; p. 20 © www.istockphoto.com/Ernest Prim; p. 29 iStockphoto/Thinkstock; p. 30 © www.istockphoto.com/TT; p. 31 © www.istockphoto.com/Neta Degany; p. 45 © Wayne Hughes/Alamy; p. 47 Matt Carr/Workbook Stock/Getty Images; pp. 50–51 © www.istockphoto.com/Steve Simzer; back cover (silhouette) Hemera/Thinkstock.

Designer: Nicole Russo; Editor: Kathy Kuhtz Campbell;
Photo Researcher: Peter Tomlinson